BREATHING IN STORMY SEASONS

BREATHING IN STORMY SEASONS

STEPHANIE GREEN

Breathing in Stormy Seasons
Recent Work Press
Canberra, Australia

Copyright © Stephanie Green, 2019

ISBN: 9780648553700(paperback)

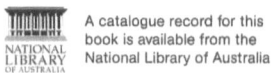 A catalogue record for this book is available from the National Library of Australia

All rights reserved. This book is copyright. Except for private study, research, criticism or reviews as permitted under the Copyright Act, no part of this book may be reproduced, stored in a retrieval system, or transmitted in any form by any means without prior written permission. Enquiries should be addressed to the publisher.

Cover image: © Ian Hutchesson 2019, featuring detail from 'Slight Uncertainty' by Michal Trpak reproduced with permission of the artist.

Cover design: Recent Work Press
Set by Charlotte Anderson with Recent Work Press

recentworkpress.com

Contents

Reconnection	1
On the train	2
Falling	3
Meeting	4
Refugee	5
Sleeping	6
Before the Uprising	7
Dancing	8
The Visitors	9
Pond	10
Shadows	11
After the Buildup	12
At High Tide	13
Bunya Pod	14
December	15
Return to Earth	16
Bush bedroom morning	17
The Catch	18
Against the Wind	19
Trees Breathe	20
Blood Moon	21
Firelight	22
Departure and Arrival	23
Pre-Memory, Papua	24
Landed	25
Keepsake	26
Tonic	27
Pine Cone Gathering, East Gippsland	28
Opening Gran's Locket	29
Memento	30
Abandoned Apartment	31
Stradbroke, Then and Now.	32
Three Things Left Behind	33
A Short Time Apart	34

Fortune	35
Scent of Past Things	36
Remembering Lake Ballard	37
The Terrible Offence	38
Indistinguishable	39
Night Sounds	40
Ending	41
Conversation	42
What can be saved	43
Scar	44
Jewel	45
On the Surface	46
Graduation Day	47
Leaving the Ninety Mile Beach	48
Remembrance	49
Cure	50
Meeting the Train	51
Nostalgia	52

Reconnection

To start again is the hardest thing, to leave behind the pock marks of memory. I think of the time I left you on the side of a road to thumb your way from east to west. There were three letters that year, each one grimy and creased from where you carried them too long. I think of the first time you came to meet my train, unexpectedly, and I had already left the station. I waited for you on the steps outside your apartment with the smell of cannelloni beans cooking somewhere nearby. There was one other time, at the airport, when you went to the wrong terminal. I stayed then too, knowing you would come.

On the train

Find your seat, stow your luggage, settle yourself. It will be a long journey. Don't look out the window until you are past the winter city. In the train you risk nothing. The faces of other travelers are mirrors of indifference. If the carriage is cold, put on your jacket, your hat, the gloves your mother knitted for you so long ago. Now you carry her memory in the knitted shell of your palm. Why the past becomes the future is a question too hard to fathom. Instead, open your book: it might keep you occupied, even though these words cannot say what needs to be said.

Leaving the winter city, it is better not to see, not to know, not to say. Perhaps when you reach the silver lake below the mountains you will have the courage to speak and the eyes of others will become kind.

Falling

It's easy to read too much and find yourself falling. The slow burn of an acid chuckle, the sod-turned ground, a thought or sentence almost out of place. The concentration required can be exhausting. In that room, that book, that time, everything still seems possible. Reading, I'm out of touch, more myself, and less, perhaps. Afterwards I'm plagued with reminders that what survives the test isn't always what lasts. Do you remember the sour ginger beer you made on the side of that Tuscan slope that had to be thrown away? Or how I had to make do with garlic as we roasted bread and tomatoes over a fire. We talked of Tristram Shandy and I wanted to write, like that, but I never would.

Meeting

It was a hot summer, an old train, late as usual. They had never met, but the compartment held them close. Narrow windows opened stiffly to the cloying air, the leather seats cracking. At every stop, dust and diesel fuel stained the air. They sat facing each other, he in his smooth American jeans, she in her Indian cotton dress. Each on their separate journeys bound for an Italian township famed for its handful of masterpieces. His eyes turned to the window and the gauzy, terraced hills. Her face was turned to a page.

He was conscious of her eyes, the fine violent veins of the lids, their lashes rising and falling and a small mole above one eyebrow that she touched lightly with her fingers. She could see his hands, brown, veins lightly distended, resting as if unaware on the arms of the opposite seat. She imagined herself turning them over and reading the lines, had she been able to tell their future. When they heard their destination announced, she looked up at him and smiled slightly.

Do they ever speak, these two? Do they visit the town together, climbing high to see the view? And, later, as the evening begins to cool, do they grasp hands at the station and run together, fast and breathless, to catch the next train?

Refugee

Whisperers in the night, a long chain composition of words and breath, chanting, as I slept, on the edge of a desert, always ready to run. Season to season, a circle, an arrow, a line, bending, a sentinel arc, an ugly rainbow, a dark line, matting the eye, a stain on dark blue, upside down, wild and uncertain, yet determined, so careful, like the bright millions moving through a plangent sky, never homeward, never gone. Now that long sigh is interrupted, the constant movement quieted. Now I can pause, listen to music, read the words of others, and dream. So everything lives again.

Sleeping

The man in the red jacket sleeps as if the sun has not risen and his bed is feather soft, one hand draped on the stone step below, the other resting on his chest. The blue sky is his only possession. He lies with his legs out straight along the step, the morning workers stepping over him to climb or descend. He sees only his dreams, no time, nothing exists but this deep-delved lethe, this stone place of rest from which he may never wake.

Before the Uprising

In Cairo, a man brushed away a rectangle of dust beside our hotel and watered the bare stem of a potted tree. On Talaat Harb the shops and cafés stayed open late into the night and people filled the street. In the laneway cafe by our hotel, men smoked their waterpipes and talked of change as we visited the ancient places thinking only of the past. The fragrance of their roasting tobacco curled over the balcony and into our room as we slept, sneaking into our dreams. In the morning, we crossed Tahrir Square and walked for hours among the markets where the stalls sold saucepans and reconditioned kettles, gleaming Dallah and bright acrylic blankets strung under a medieval bridge. A young woman stopped the storm surge of hostile cars for us with a gesture and a boy danced as he carried cups of chai on a metal tray. Through the window of a bus, I saw a man crack a whip over a thin donkey as it dragged a cart. A young cat ran towards us along a cobbled lane, its white fur stained grey, hoping for food or water. A girl wearing a pretty hijab showed me how I should fold my own scarf behind my head. Later, my fingers couldn't remember the feel of how to tie the knot, but I remembered the grit of the desert between my fingers and did not hurry to brush it away.

Dancing

Boys stamping at pigeons on a windy street. A woman combing her long red hair then turning her delicate face towards an ambulance's wailing cry. Girls smiling for each other as they pose beside stony remains. A wall that could not last. A couple eating ice cream as they walk through courtyards, pale walls patterned with green, tangled vines. Two friends reminding each other that there are times to forget, to look away from grey stained blocks of stone and to feel the fine spray of the fountain on our cheeks, before we leave.

The Visitors

Don't listen. Shut your door. Close the window and don't look out. If you see, look away. Shut down the computer. Switch off the lights. Turn off the taps, the stove. Close your eyes. Say nothing. Wait. Sit quietly, as if you were nowhere, knowing nothing. As if you did not exist. They say the world is a harsh place. They say there is not enough for us to share. Punish the ones who refuse their suffering. Punish the dispossessed who spill over our borders. They will take our homes, our offices. Keep them out, they say. Keep them in. Or, we too will be dispossessed. But sometimes you can't help hearing. Or wondering, after all, what you would do. For what we hold to ourselves is no more than air, and we are all visitors here. So, sometimes, you can't sit still enough. And, sometimes, after all, you can't stay quiet.

Pond

The sky opens and your mirror surface fractures, pointilist, wet-needled, green-fringed. Later you will seep away to the thick places, stirring the earth and for a while, quick-fingered, I will forget you. If I lay down here on the wet grass and forgot myself, leaves would cover my body and I too would flow into your belonging, let my words go, like twigs falling dry from the restless forest, tracing only a line on the bright plane of your soft silt, as the frogs and tadpoles, brief in their passing.

Shadows

In the shadows you are as quick as a cat, slipping through doorways, between corners, your whisper so soft and light I could almost forget you. I feel your breath on my neck, just at that place where you used to lick me, afterwards, tasting salt and blowing gently to make me cool again. In the shadows, through the slippage of summer sight, I can almost see you, flicking your plait like a tapered tail as you climb through the line of trees. In the shadows, sun fades as if evening had already fallen and maybe all I have to do is listen.

After the Buildup

Almost summer and the air has been pushed out by a thick grey sky. Nothing breathes. Even the giant palm hands are folded quietly. The flowering Jacarandas never waver, misted in purple and breathlessly reaching for the sky. We expect nothing and the day passes somehow, me at my grandmother's old desk, scratched with time; you creeping in now and then with a plea for me to remember the words you forget. At the end of this silver white day the light has barely changed. Only at sunset when the neighbours start shouting over the floral metal fence, do we go out to see if we can clear the air again.

At High Tide

Near the water's edge you can still see to the bottom. Small fish school my toes, swishing their silver feather tails. Further out, three women keep their heads above water, speaking of other days. Under the surface, the lagoon is deep and thick with salt. My sight is cloaked. I swim for the other side, blinded, through yellow-green, lured by the sandbank's golden glow. Every few strokes I lift my head above the surface to check my direction, blinking into clarity. My feet feel for firmness, the sand slips away, but I am not looking to land.

Bunya Pod

You are a pentagram, a glorious tawny shield. An impossible flower of iron, a Medieval five-fingered vice. Armoured and spiky, your fierce studded fertility clasps to time, keeping close what must grow. In the warm wet season of openings and beginnings, these tapered claws open to let fall the secret seed into the world. Then you become a fallen shell, a dry palm cupped in a gesture of care, a wary welcome to country. Air, water and light surround you. It will take a long time for your beauty to dry and fade. If they let your seed grow in this forest, the tree will be long-lived and tall. If they let the tree stand in this forest, it will draw other creatures to itself. Admiring they will touch the rough surface of the bark, scarred from its living. Hungry, they will climb your thick curling limbs and feed together at your feet. Then, fallen, scattered, you may begin again.

December

The dry winds of early summer scatter dead leaves to my door. We are aimless this season, except that I have rearranged the patterned rugs and patched the fly wire screen door: a small measure of protection. Yesterday, I dug holes in the weed-infested lawn and planted handfuls of seeds hoping for a crop of soft grass for the cat to nibble or recline upon. We donated the television set long ago in one of the Council's annual collections. I hope one day to see it displayed in a museum of past things. Now we sit on the blue-tiled porch and swap stories, imagining we are Hansel and Gretel making our way through the dark woods of trouble, crumbling gingerbread traces between our fingers, hoping one day we can find our way back.

Return to Earth

Hobbled these days, I bury myself in the earth of these remaining forests. Rain sharpens my appetite, sweetens my breath. I bare my claws and burrow down into the rich, musty, dampness, below softening pine needles, below the fine fibres and roots, slipping between their complex systems, until I am hidden in soft darkness. There the quiet buzz of myriad life muffles the roar of war. There, thoughts are fertile. There death is everything and nothing.

Bush bedroom morning

Outside my window the water's surface shifts lightly, depths dark under the patina of green. Wind's breath, mosquito ferment. A heron lands, almost silently, screwing its white neck to the shadowy pool like an unexpected call from a stranger. At night the frogs utter a clipped counterpoint interrupting the singing insects, aquatic cascade. They are a kind of company when anything else seems impossible, or when we are unbidden, as we must all sometimes be. But now the early sunlight winds through the door drawing me to the warmth outside, to a view of the mown valley and I am unable to refuse.

The Catch

At first they seem nothing more than a small cloud of dust propelled out of dawn, passing over the cliffs and out beyond the purple cove. Closer now they are some kind of wave, animated angles rising and falling against the rose blue sky, full of pace and noise and flourish. And then they become hundreds, crying out to each other as they rush towards me. I am breathless, surrounded, amidst a fury of great wings trapping and sweeping the air. Bodies thump against me as I breathe in down and dust from a million feathers, my skin savaged by the thrust of claws and beaks. I am about to be cast down. I am not one of them. Yet as the air falls away, as the ocean rises and I fall helpless towards the depths, they still have me in their grasp.

Against the Wind

Against the wind, the limbs of trees sing like open sea, green waves moving against granite sky. From outside, you called to me and I could not hear you. Do you remember the rain on the metal roof? And the grey storm crackling and howling? So loud I thought I must be alone, but you were at the door soaking wet with rain. I listened for the fissures of sound and at last let you in. That night we listened to the radio, the music harsh and wild, as we made omelettes over a small gas flame and spoke of the past. Like the lonely storm wind, I wanted to cry. Later, you read to me from something you'd written, an homage to Neruda you said, although I could not have told how. But we were alive, and then the night was sweet and still.

Trees Breathe

A decade ago I had a mind to cut down a tree in my front yard, disliking its thin reaching trunk, its poor, dry twigs and adumbrated branches, reaching so far above my head. Years later, sheer laziness having saved the tree from being felled, I saw the beginnings of magnificence, its branches feathering at last against the sky. So much time and space a tall, young being needs, to fill out, to breathe enough to grow and become itself. Trees share sweet breath, as if we would share too. With them we are everything. Without them we are wraiths walking a small, dead plastic world.

Blood Moon

On the night of the bleeding moon we go outside to look up, but the street is empty and the trees are sparkling with rain. Only the remnant of a glow shines through thick cloud. It would have been nice to see it, we say to each other, wishing for a moment we were in San Francisco or Bangkok and not alone. Later we will marvel at so many eyes turned to the sky and wish for the days of miracles. There's always another eclipse you remind me, taking my arm as we go inside, to bed.

Firelight

Once there were matches that could strike on anything. A promise of sparks igniting dangerous possibilities, fiery rebellions, outspoken words at the very least. Safety was out of the question until the match girls marched in the streets for suffrage and more. Maybe, like me, you grew up with the scent of phosphorous and smoke in your nostrils, the vivid splash against a rough paper flint, and the hiss of gas ready to take fire. It's rare now, except for a candle on a birthday evening, lit from a faded red matchbox kept in the high kitchen cupboard. But the other night, when the power went dark, and no one was quite sure what to do next, it was all you had to light your way.

Departure and Arrival

I was born to travel, leaving one island for another, unknowing in my mother's arms as we made our way south. I had no memory of the brown rush basket she carried me in as a tiny baby, 4.2lbs, or the lilting of ship and train that brought us from Port Moresby to Brisbane. She said later it was the only time in my first six months I didn't cry, as if I could only be content in transit. Now, I cherish the promise of disheveled sidings, the untidy industry of tide-blown ports, warehouses lit up with graffiti, a rush of green or blue past a window, lakesides strewn with holiday debris, hurried crowds waiting to board. I am there with each passing moment and gone again, collecting the pieces and leaving them behind, yet no trace ever lost.

Pre-Memory, Papua

What were you to me but a flimsy screen door slamming at the end of a wooden corridor, leaving me nothing but half-remembered dreams? In the mornings, I only knew the rising sun that silenced the noise of the insects. In the afternoons, I only knew you brought coolness and rain, as women ran to turn louvres or snatch washing from makeshift lines. I never walked in your forests or sat under a giant flame tree with my basket. I never wore frangipani flowers in my hair. If the first voice I knew was my mother's, it was yours that later brought me to tears, as you sang stories in the lilt of your own language. If the arms that held me carried me from you to another land, I never forgot your embraces: the scent of mango, dancing fire smoke or the soft kiss of a harbour breeze, full of longing to return.

Landed

You can't talk to me yet. I am too small to understand you, but I know that only a few days off the ship you're impatient, wondering where we will settle. At first the bare limbed frangipani makes you homesick for PNG and your own garden scented with ripe mango and tropical flowers. You miss the tall trees and the great tangle of vines that surrounded your house, softening the heat and buzzing with animal life. Yet, as the days pass you begin to long for the places buried deep in your own childhood: a thin curling road to a farm house gate, flat sheep-strewn paddocks, and the smell of eucalyptus leaves on a cool wet day. Soon, you will take us there and some part of me will never belong anywhere else.

Keepsake

A long time ago, you beckoned me in under the temple arches to escape the rain and here we stood together looking west. The sky brightened but still we did not leave. Since then we have walked on the northern moors. You climbed a hill and took photographs while I sat under a rock and wrote poems. The forest trees were a still measure of our passing. I say to you, if I write a post card to you, keep it for me. But you say, why keep what you can live?

Tonic

At the age of eight I almost stopped eating. First the green and yellow vegetables, then the potatoes and meat, so that my hair thinned and my bones began to show through. My mother said I could not live on ice cream and toast and took me to our family doctor, a soft, dark haired man with a high nasal voice, as if he was speaking through a straw. He talked to my mother in a soft inexplicable rush as I counted the different kinds of cold; the grey floor, the metal edge of the table, the doctor's hand, the sharp needle, and floating between us some nuance of disapproval I could never fathom, hers or his, or mine perhaps, each sure in her or his own way that this cold practice would keep all of us safe.

Afterwards, he prescribed Scott's Emulsion, opening the big jar of multi-coloured jelly beans that sat on his desk. He asked me which colours I liked best. 'All of them', I said, pushing my tongue against the gaps in my milk teeth. He poured them from a scoop into my hand and I saved them, clutched in my rainbow-stained fist, to eat one by one at the kitchen table, biting them in half and chewing slowly to make them last.

Every morning, after we saw the doctor, my father poured Scott's Emulsion into a battered silver-plate spoon and held it out eagerly until I opened my mouth like a bird. Sometimes I told him I did not need to be fed with a spoon. I had started school. I could do it myself. But he insisted, one strand of brown hair curled down over his forehead as he smiled and nodded at me. He would spend decades trying to plaster it back, until his hairline receded and the greying curl disappeared.

Pine Cone Gathering, East Gippsland

In the winter I collected pine cones for my mother on a farm where the old bush was once razed. The tall brown and green trees that sucked life from the soil. She dried the pine cones and used them every morning to start our wood fire. When the green cones turned brown and opened their scales, I would shake out the seeds and collect them in a white enamel mug. Year after year, I wanted to plant the seeds to see if any would grow. Year after year, the seeds stayed on my window sill until the pods cracked dry, full of cobwebs and dust. My mother made me throw them out, shaking her grey head at my neglect. I could have cleaned those seeds of the tall trees that never belonged. I could have polished the seeds with wax or resin. I could have sewn them together with silver thread, linking each seed to each, to coil in my palm, and remember.

Opening Gran's Locket

You will be forever a fair child, my long dead, Aunt Grace, Gran's first daughter, dead of diphtheria at twelve years old. She kept you chained at her heart her whole life and you never once complained. I spring the delicate catch and it's as if she has stepped out to join me, unburied, spiriting her loneliness into a pale cloud, dust on my clothes. I could curl up with you inside this gold locket with your faded yellow curls, bringing with me your treasured white alabaster bowl and three favourite novels bound in tooled leather. No one would ever find me, except you, your grey cherished face smiling and reminding me of what can never be lost.

Memento

Years ago, he sent me a picture of a door, its green paint cracked and peeling from the weather, with a black wrought umbrella handle ready to be turned. He'd printed it during the last age on photographic paper, stained, with a flat crease at one corner as if it had been stuck under a pile of books on the edge of his dining table for too long. His note said the door was made long ago from pieces of the broken bridge, cracked during a storm at the time of the last revolution, when the flat land flooded to the sea. If it was a famous door, or his door, or some kind of invitation, there were no words to say. I took it as a memento of our lost time together, something he wanted me to frame and hang in the corridor, beside the brown corner bookcase with its dusty family burdens, so that I would see it daily in passing and always wonder.

Abandoned Apartment

A mist of dust and cobwebs, silverfish trails and peeling paint, the ceiling plaster falling in drifts. I could write words on every surface with the tip of my finger. Underneath the debris is a life once lived, memories left behind but never quite forgotten. Here is the worn guitar, silent now for so many years. Here are the books you wanted me to bring – 'references', I think you said, but to me they are more like old friends you've missed. And here is the familiar photograph of your grandmother with her shopping bag, sitting next to you at a bus stop in her warm pink coat and you wearing your favourite woollen jumper. She seems about to say something to you. I wonder if you remember what it was?

Stradbroke, Then and Now.

If you grew up in the country of summer holidays, Stradbroke is an island in a bay, now a place of escape for city dwellers, its beautiful cliffs and blue coves once stolen from its people, dug into, occupied, stranded by globalisation's high tides. But, for me, Stradbroke is another place. A swathe of bush paddocks in remote East Gippsland, white and black sandy tracks through thick bracken, the smell of banksia and eucalyptus, smoke from the billy fire. There in perpetuity my uncle is straining fence wire and whistling at the dogs. There my brother loses grandpa's hammer amongst the tussocks as I collect wood, and a black stone axe is unearthed in my hand after centuries of buried time.

Three Things Left Behind

The day after the funeral, I stand in the kitchen and count cubic centimetres on my fingers and toes, wondering what I can bear to keep, and what I can bear to leave behind. So much to slip through my fingers, with rain and wind. Years later I regret everything and nothing. The small etched crystal jug with its lid broken in two, glued together with a father's cracked fingers. Once a year we filled it with homemade vinaigrette and set it down on Gran's lace table-cloth as if she were still alive to approve. The silver tea pot, blackened and bent, that a mother filled with tea and careful hot water after lunches and funerals. Once a year she polished it with Silvo and rags, sitting at the back room dining table in the morning sun as if the years and mornings would never end. And the old painted sewing cupboard with its fold-down table, that rested, flimsy, on one leg. Once a year we pulled out the old Singer sewing machine to make seams and hems as if all our stitches would keep us together.

A Short Time Apart

You send me a portrait of our cat poised to leap from that pile of books I stacked on my desk before I came away. Four paws together, tail up like a sail tapped to the wind. Those editions of Trollope and Meredith, beneath some modern paperbacks. Stein, of course, Faulkner and Hemingway. Woolf's essays and a novel by Compton-Burnett I once read to you aloud. The Eliot I gave away last spring but Bowen is still there, along with a couple of slim volumes, one French, the other Russian. There she is, our beauty, coat sleek and golden, ears and nose pointing forward, perfectly balanced on that slippery tower. Almost already in flight, at any moment the tower will topple as she leaps.

Fortune

They say it's bad luck to drive through a swarm of bees, and so it was. Seven years of sadness and beauty. In exile, I lived beside a wide silver river that curled through loss, sand and strangeness. Every morning I leaned into a hot inland wind, forcing myself towards the west against nothing I could name. Dust blew into my lungs from distant quarries and eroded plains and I welcomed it, although fearing its aftermath, because it reminded me that nothing stays the same. Every afternoon the sea winds blew me back towards the east, cool salt gobbets of air that tested my resolve. Seven years later I flew east with that wind, brushing the grit from my hands as I came home.

Scent of Past Things

Twenty years since the final meeting, an obstacle course in parallel with separate entrances and exits. I can't remember the last letter – an act of will perhaps – only that I folded it up into four squares and put it on my top kitchen shelf, a place I could not see or easily reach. I left it in that place for a year before lighting a candle and sending those forgotten words into a universe of unknowing, a pale thread of smoke that faded slowly. If I caught its trace in the room afterwards I opened a window or filled a vase with stolen rosemary and lavender, to cover the scent of the desert between us.

Remembering Lake Ballard

After sun is the black time, when each of us is blind and alone. In that moment I think you are lost to me, wandering the muddy floor of an ancient lake below a volcanic hill. I can't see the mud or the hill or the beings that inhabit this dark. There are no sounds, shapes or colours, no others to share the loss. Even the air is still, and so dry I can't taste the last of my own saliva. We are the black sky and the silence, waiting for the stars that come without warning to touch our eyes.

The Terrible Offence

That summer day, I sat on the polite white sofa with your mother and pretended I knew no French in case I stumbled, again, to be corrected. She said, unexpectedly, how you had hurt her. A decade ago. Some neglect that revealed something about you I could not yet fathom. She said she would never forgive you for it, any more than she would forgive me for taking up with you 'in sin'. What kind of future would we have? I could say nothing. She repeated the story, how you abandoned her all those years ago. As if I had not heard it the first time, sitting so close beside her, her champagne breath, already bitter, in my nostrils. I felt the flick of her furious silver blonde hair, so much like Dietrich in exile. I watched her stiff hands moving in air, crippled by age as I sat quiet and looked down at my own tight-folded fingers. In other circumstances I might have started to hum quietly to myself. Instead, silently, I began to list those few phrases in French I could still remember - *je suis, je sais* - until your mother changed the subject, or poured the coffee, or opened another bottle of champagne. At last we drank, speaking of nothing but blue boats in the harbor or pink light on the risen river, until the afternoon slipped away, and you disappeared from our thoughts with the wind.

Indistinguishable

In another, more adventurous, time we walked the high ridge between forest and ocean, darkness and light moving across a laden sky. And when the onslaught came, we weathered under the mountain and you kissed me as if it would last. That night I read to you from Proust and you did not listen, but long afterwards you made me tiny Madeleines which pricked my mouth with sweetness. When I had been ill and my face was pale as calla lilies, you took me in your arms and I could feel your heart beating, as if fearfully. But, on the last day, you kissed me under the climbing roses in your mother's garden. Their wet red petals caressed my cheek, their thorns tore my lips, and I could not tell the difference.

Night Sounds

Sometimes you stay awake for the muffled sounds of night: white seagulls crying overhead, a hiss of leaves, or a distant engine stirring. Sometimes, the neighbours rehearse their song for the last performance of their lives, *que sera sera*. He wears a sombrero and she will carry a fan, red and black, red and black. The disappointed cat leaps sleekly from the roof onto a narrow brick wall and slips past your window. You have to listen very hard to hear it, but in the morning when you wake, it will be waiting.

Ending

That last time at the airport I kissed him, but my lips were hard with cold and we were nothing more than two marionettes bumping faces politely. He gripped my arms and looked hard into my eyes without speaking, the wordlessness too heavy to translate. That time, I patted his shoulder with my gloved hand, feeling the cold seams pressing along my fingers. He shrugged away, dog-like, uninterested in pats or kisses, ready to leave for somewhere warm.

Conversation

In Morocco we put down our books and swallow cupfuls of mint tea, wishing the cups were bigger. We are thirsty for something else but neither of us will say what it is. Instead we reach for the salt to sting our tongues, something sharp and familiar in this strange time. There's a feint of wind and we think there's movement, but still the conversation stays the same, circling the unspoken.

What can be saved

At first we threw them out, thinking there'd be more, that there'd always be enough. Now we take them in, little fugitives from a careless world. We store them in bowls and cups, on trays and in drawers, in case we need them later or just because it would be a waste to throw them away. It's easy not to notice, to let them slip through as if they don't matter, but we do our best. Sometimes it gets a little crowded but we don't mind. I like to leave them lying around, on the kitchen bench or the dining table, in small tangled loops and crisscrossed lines, comforting in their loose untidiness, their readiness to be of use.

Scar

There is an invisible claw across my face that never lets me go, a web that burns and never heals. Every day it reminds me skin is testimony, lined, stretched, pitted, worn. My skin may not record where your hand glides, smooth-soft, feeling its expert way to my core. It may not remember the warm swell of meeting flesh or the wet touch of your kiss. But this thin cloak for blood and sinew shows how it is torn: a pane of falling glass, a surgeon's knife, a careless cut, or the red scarring of a burn. Whatever else, I am knitted together by its claims.

Jewel

In the café with blue spider tiles I dangle my feet and watch the girl carry cups with red-nosed smile, sniffing into handkerchief between customers. She knows the value, hard work for a living, olive apron ironed, fingers clasping shiny pendant, smoothed silk black hair bob bristling fibres in humid air. She pats the new girl's shoulder lightly as if to reassure, or her own solace, a reminder of kindness? Stained by the big hotel shadow, three café tables and bench with stools. The narrow stand with sugar and cinnamon that's mostly just for show. I perch with my bitter-sweet coffee and wonder if I'll be back. If I come often, order Sumatra coffee and truffle fries, eating them slowly one by one as if it comes naturally, some day, maybe, it will.

On the Surface

I once heard Kafka say that it's the rules that keep us at the surface of things. He called me from the deck of a small seismic vessel while taking soundings on the Brisbane water and trying to keep the pilot from sailing out to sea. Afterwards I wondered how Kafka manages to be so precise and so profound at the same time. I guess, if I asked him, he would laugh and say that depth is a matter for the birds.

Graduation Day

If she sees me she doesn't show it. Her eyes are all for the centre stage. Tall heels, short white skirt under the heavy black gown, red hair streaming under the pointed hard hat. It's no protection but it says something about how far she's come. She wobbles slightly, as she approaches, on those narrow heels, but she's in too much of a hurry to let uncertainty slow her down. She might think I'm somewhere amongst those other black gowned fellows or she might never think of me again, ready to shed the shroud.

Leaving the Ninety Mile Beach

Picaresque, you say as you pick up your duffel bag and sling it onto the rusted corrugations of the utility tray. The driver hasn't heard the word before but he doesn't flinch. Just puts the ute in gear and lets the handbrake go, sweetly. He's heading inland to Shepparton. You tell him you might pick up some work there. What're you looking for mate, he says, and you tell him anything, anything at all. You can't think of what else to say so the two of you settle into your seats, eyes on the yellow paddocks. It's been days since you talked to anyone, hanging out on the ninety-mile beach with a fishing rod, nothing but white bread for bait, and the last of the beer. Ninety miles between you and the future. With the power in the shack finally cut off you listened to the waves sighing and thudding as the sun set over a coal fired horizon. A long cold night stoking the rusted pot belly stove. You knew it was time to go. You'll miss the sea, you say, and the driver nods. There are inlanders and coast dwellers, he shrugs. He doesn't say which one he belongs to but it's a long way to Shepparton and a lot can happen between there and here.

Remembrance

Two men at the Harbourtown market cafe, meat pies on plates, tiny orange china cups pinched between forefinger and thumb, arthritic opposable, thickened with work and age. One groomed and tidy, his white hair smooth waves: the other unshaved, knitted jacket slipping from a red-singleted shoulder. One nods, then the other. One puts the cup down, quietly observing a ritual that's, maybe, decades old. I remember my parents sitting like this at the Bulleen shopping centre cafe, thirty years or more ago, with a slice of raison bread and a large pot of tea as the old men gathered and gossip, waiting for their wives under dull neon lights to warm the day and remember the old world, the familiarity of change. I remember the talk of those times, although I listened only to the rustle of the river. Now I too have become a watcher and a wistful gossip, longing for comforts.

Cure

He goes up to the roof sometimes, after midnight. It's the only time and place he can think. Somehow the black pinnacles of the Norfolk pines, moving softly with the sea air, make him feel a little less lonely. Once, unable to fall asleep at 3am, he went up wearing his navy-blue cotton pajamas. Half way down the lift jammed, its buttons refusing to respond. He could have pressed the alarm button to call Security, but instead lay down on the floor, curled up like a cat and slept. Only the lift, coming to life of its own accord, woke him at 6am as it descended with the gentle ease of a hovercraft. Whenever he can't sleep now, after midnight, he gets into the lift with a pillow, curls up in a corner and closes his eyes. It's the only time when the threat that someone might find him can't keep him awake.

Meeting the Train

His purple Hawaiian shirt was too thin for the cold afternoon. His embrace stained with the beer, sweat and cigarettes. I still thought of him as the handsome, blue-eyed boy I'd grown up with, in the distant days of scrapes and adventures. As a shearer, moving with the seasons, he'd turn up at my place with a bag full of dirty clothes and some wild story to tell. At the age of twenty-two he'd already been right around Australia, working odd jobs for contractors and station managers. When the job came to an end, he'd turn up at a pub and talk to the locals about who might have work for cash. In the Gulf country he got sick drinking from dirty water holes after his van broke down. He shot wild horses from a helicopter. Once, he was gaoled for drunk driving in some remote border town. It was just the two policemen and him. In the afternoons they let him out of the pen to play cricket in the police station corridor. They used a rubbish bin for a wicket, stuffed full of bags of marijuana they'd seized from some unlucky fool. On the last night, the three of them shared a joint and Chinese takeaway from the only restaurant in town. After, they locked him up again but, in the morning, they let him go without charge. He thought maybe they'd only picked him up in the first place because they were lonely and bored. Now, he has only the stories to tell and me to write them down.

Nostalgia

Even if you believe that time is a river, there's no going back to that white slick of sand or the worn knotted rope over the waterhole that the boys swung and leapt from in summer, the brown bread sandwiches and the hot sweet tea smelling of all the times your mother has made tea in that thermos before, or the hot ripples of brown shade and the treacherous tree trunk islands beckoning us through the ripples, until the prick of mosquitoes surrounded us at dusk.

Afterword

Some years ago, Professor Kevin Brophy referred to the poet T.S. Eliot's explanation of his translation from a French prose poem by John Perse. Its 'abbreviation of method' could be justified, he suggested, by how 'the sequence of images coincides and concentrates into one intense impression' (Eliot 1975 qtd in Brophy 2002). Brophy uses Eliot's account of the writing of a prose poem to make a larger case for the form, elaborating aspects of its cultural and literary historiography, describing it as 'a brief and brilliant aphoristic flare in the general darkness around us', akin to philosophy (2002). He goes much further, however, for while Eliot observes, somewhat legalistically, that the prose poem's 'arrangement of imagery requires just as much fundamental brainwork as the arrangement of an argument' (1975), Brophy sets out, just as argumentatively - although less legalistically -, to show how the writing of a prose poem 'moves by feel' (2002). Brophy concludes, definitively, in poetic form, with the image of a tightrope-walker 'who fell silent' from the rope, so that the audience is left facing the shocking emptiness of the reality, captured in a final image: the realisation of 'their own futures scattered across the sawdust like so many minor constellations, a vision of static' (2002).

It is this kind of confrontation between the shock of materiality and the sensitivity of imaginative apprehension that resonates with my approach to the making of the prose poems in this collection. Rather than seeking to redefine a poetic form that has been already endlessly defined by others, the claims of this work lie in the realm of engagement with the elusivity and viscera of being, and the interplay between them.

Jen Webb refers to poetry as, among other things, an act of 'bearing witness' (2012, 8). I would argue for the prose poem as way of capturing the momentary experience of being in time and space. Merleau-Ponty argues that the body is the point of reference for everything we what we do, feel and experience (1945/2012). This is perhaps doubly so for the female body, which, as Franks points out, remains 'a contested space' (2016).

Walter Benjamin remarks in *One Way Street* that any human effort is 'impeded in its unfolding by the boundless resistance of the outside world' (1978, 75). Prose poetry can capture the force of this resistance, its materiality and imperviousness to subjectivity, but also its pause and, through memory, its constant change. These prose poems – I would like to call them 'moments of poetry' – recall journeys and intimacies, spaces of habitation, daily practices of denial, rescue, affection or assertion. They reflect on negotiations between body and mind that can so fiercely mark the experience of womanhood, striving to capture the intermittent intensity of this 'boundless resistance' through the impact of summer and winter storms.

Works Cited

Benjamin, W. 1978. One Way Street. In *Reflections: Essays, Aphorisms, Autobiographies*. Ed. Peter Demetz. Trans. Edmond Jephcott. London: Harcourt, Brace, Jovanovich: 61-90.

Brophy, K. 2002. The prose poem: A short history, a brief reflection and a dose of the real thing. *TEXT Journal* 6.1 April 2002: http://www.textjournal.com.au/april02/brophy.htm

Eliot, T. S. 1975. *Selected Prose of T. S. Eliot*. Ed. Frank Kermode. London: Faber and Faber.

Franks, R. 2016. A woman's place: constructing women within true crime narratives. In *TEXT Journal* Special Issue 34: Writing and illustrating interdisciplinary research. Eds Simon Dwyer, Rachel Franks, Monica Galassi and Kirsten Thorpe: http://www.textjournal.com.au/speciss/issue34/Franks.pdf

Merleau-Ponty, M. 1945/2012. Trans. DA Landes. *Phenomenology of Perception*. Oxford: Routledge.

Webb, J. 2012. Seeing, doing, knowing: Poetry and the pursuit of knowledge. *TEXT Journal* Special Issue 13: Creativity: Cognitive, Social and Cultural Perspectives. Eds. Nigel McLoughlin & Donna Lee Brien: http://www.textjournal.com.au/speciss/issue13/Webb.pdf

Acknowledgements

Many of these prose poems were written for, or inspired by, the International Prose Poetry Project. I therefore thank Paul Hetherington and all the project contributors for their creativity and comradeship. I must give special acknowledgement to Shane Strange, for his clear-sighted and stalwart editorship for which I am deeply grateful. A warm note of appreciation to Cassandra Atherton and Ian Hutchesson for their encouragement and their generous and attentive reading of the original manuscript. Thanks also to the Directors of The Cooroora Institute, Tamsin Kerr and Ross Annels, for the great gift of an Artist-in-Residency (2018) which enabled me to develop this manuscript.

Previously published:

'To start again is the hardest thing'. Originally published as untitled prose poem. *TEXT Journal* Special Issue 46. Prose Poetry'. Edited by Monica Carroll, Shane Strange and Jen Webb: http://www.textjournal.com.au/speciss/issue46/Green_poetry.pdf

'Reconnection'. Originally published as an untitled contribution to the Prose Poetry Project Anthology, *Pulse: Prose Poems*. Eds Shane Strange and Monica Carroll. Recent Work Press, 2016.

'Nostalgia', Originally published as untitled untitled contribution to the Prose Poetry Project Anthology, *Tract: Prose Poems*. Eds Paul Munden and Monica Carroll. University of WA Press. Oct 2017. Recent Work Press, 2017, p. 21.

Biographical Note

Stephanie Green is an Australian writer and academic. Her creative work includes short fiction, poetry, essays and cultural journalism, published in journals such as *Axon, TEXT Journal, Griffith Review, Overland*, and a variety of anthologies and collections. Her writing has been recognised in numerous literary awards, including The Age Short Story Award (1991) and the Hal Porter Short Story Award (2012). She published a collection of short fiction entitled *Too Much Too Soon* with Pandanus Press in 2006 and a selection of her poetry, *Shadow Memories*, has been produced as catalogue, to accompany an exhibition of associated drawings by Melbourne artist James Yuncken (Insula, 2015). She also contributes to the International Prose Poetry Project.

Stephanie teaches writing in the School of Humanities, Languages and Social Science at Griffith University, where she is Program Director for the Graduate Certificate in Creative and Professional Writing. Her academic books and journal articles include studies in creative writing, biography, literary and screen culture, including, *The Public Lives of Charlotte and Marie Stopes* (London: Pickering & Chatto, 2013), 'Romanticism and Contemporary Australian Writing' *TEXT Journal* Special Issue 41 (edited with Paul Hetherington, 2017) and 'The Deflected Subject: ethics, objects and writing,' *Axon Journal* 2 (2012).

2019 Editions

Palace of Memory: An elegy **Paul Hetherington**
Acting Like a Girl **Sandra Renew**
A Coat of Ashes **Jackson**
Summer Haiku **Owen Bullock**
A Common Garment **Anita Patel**
Giant Steps: Reflections on Apollo 11 and beyond **Various**
Some Sketchy Notes on Matter **Angela Gardner**
Canberra Light **Paul Cliff**
A Wardrobe of Selves **Peter Bakowski**
Breathing in Stormy Seasons **Stephanie Green**
Strange Creatures **Alyson Miller**

2018 Editions

The Uncommon Feast **Eileen Chong**
Inlandia **KA Nelson**
Peripheral Vision **Martin Dolan**
The Love of the Sun **Matt Hetherington**
Moving Targets **Jen Webb**
Things I Have Thought to Tell You Since I Saw You Last **Penelope Layland**
The Many Uses of Mint **Ravi Shankar**
Abstractions **Various**
ACE: Arresting, Contemporary stories by Emerging Writers **Various**

all titles available from
www.recentworkpress.com

www.ingramcontent.com/pod-product-compliance
Lightning Source LLC
Chambersburg PA
CBHW030529010526
44110CB00048B/1039